P9-CBE-354

Greatest Heroes and Legends OF THE BIBLE

David and Goliath

retold by K.S. Rodriguez
illustrated by Mary Kurnick Maass

inchworm
PRESS
™

King Saul was the first king of Israel. God was unhappy with King Saul because he had disobeyed him. Saul was more concerned with making his subjects happy than he was in following the will of God.

God told the prophet Samuel, "King Saul has turned away from me. So I have chosen another to be the future king of Israel. He is one of Jesse's sons. Go to Bethlehem to bless the new king. Tell Jesse and his family that you have come to make a sacrifice to me — they do not need to know the real reason."

Samuel journeyed to Bethlehem to bless the future king. The townspeople were fearful that such a great seer was visiting them. "Is God displeased with us? Are you bringing bad news?" the people asked.

"My good people of Bethlehem, I have come here only to make sacrifices to our Lord. I wish you all peace," said Samuel, assuring the crowd.

Later that day, Samuel found Jesse and seven of his sons working in the fields. Jesse lined up his sons, oldest to youngest. Samuel looked over each son carefully. They were all strong, handsome men. Then God said, "Samuel, all of Jesse's sons are not here. Go find the youngest son, David."

Samuel found David in the meadow. David was playing the harp for his sheep, and the smallest of the flock, Curly, was asleep on his lap. David was such a thin, young boy! Samuel couldn't believe David was the one God had chosen.

"Do not look upon his youth and size," God advised Samuel, "but into his heart. Go and bless the next king of Israel." And Samuel gave the spirit of God to David, Jesse's youngest son.

One day, David's older brothers were called to battle the Philistines. David desperately wanted to join his brothers, but they only mocked him. "You're too small to fight. Stay home with Papa. Play with your harp and your sheep," his oldest brother Eliab said.

"One day you'll see how brave I really am!" cried David to his brothers. Then, he marched up the mountain path with his herd of sheep. As he walked, he picked up stones and placed them in his satchel. Curly struggled over a boulder and David gave him a helpful push. Curly beamed happily and nuzzled David's hand.

It was nighttime when they reached the green pasture at the top of the mountain. David fell asleep under a tree, and Curly and the rest of the flock were scattered on the meadow, sleeping peacefully.

They did not see the two gold eyes glowing in the shadows. A mountain lion had crept toward the meadow dotted with sleeping sheep.

The lion raised his head from behind a tall patch of grass and snarled. The sheep woke up, bleating frantically. The lion swiped and pounced, but the sheep escaped. All except for Curly who was standing alone and shaking with fear.

Curly charged off and the lion effortlessly leapt over him, blocking his path. Curly stumbled and turned in the opposite direction but again, the lion flew over him and landed right in front of him! Curly fearfully backstepped as the lion cornered him against the mountain wall. Curly was trapped!

The lion roared forcefully and David's eyes flew open. "Curly?" he cried. David jumped up, grabbing his staff and his sling shot. He ran like the wind to the sound of the lion's roar. The lion swiped at Curly with his big paws, and Curly ducked and moaned. Still running, David twirled his sling shot. "God, guide my hand. Make my aim be true," he cried. The rock smacked the lion square in the head, sending him tumbling to the ground, dead.

The next morning when David returned home, his father wanted him to bring some food to his brothers at the battlefield.

"Father, can I join them? Can I fight at their side? Last night, I fought a lion with my sling and staff! I was scared, but I knew God would protect me."

"That's quite a tale, David. But you needn't invent stories to impress me. I know you are very brave," said Jesse.

"But, but—" David stammered.

"That's enough, son. Go to the battlefield and bring your brothers some food."

How surprised David's brothers were to see him! "Did you think we'd let you fight with us?" asked Eliab. "Go home now, David. You could get hurt."

Suddenly, a voice bellowed through the valley. The men scrambled to see what was going on. Standing in the valley was the largest man they had ever seen. He was a giant! He towered above everyone else, and his arms and legs resembled thick tree trunks.

"I am Goliath of Gath!"
he shouted, raising his boulder-
sized fist into the air. His
chest was as wide and thick as
a stone wall. His long red
beard looked like it belonged
to the devil. A curved blade
was slung over his shoulder,
and a double-edged sword
hung from his side.

"Send your bravest, strongest warrior to fight me in the valley. If your champion is victorious, we shall surrender and be your slaves!" The ground shook from Goliath's thunderous voice. He pounded his giant spear on the ground and shouted, "But if I am victorious, you shall surrender and be our slaves!"

The Israelite troops were silent. King Saul stepped forward and pleaded to his men. "I offer great riches and my daughter's hand in marriage to the man who brings me Goliath's head. Surely among you is a brave warrior who will fight the giant!" Saul cried. No man accepted the challenge.

Finally, David spoke up. "Send me."

The King couldn't believe the young boy was the only one willing to fight. "Is this some kind of joke?" he asked incredulously.

"Since no one else wants to," David responded, "I shall face the giant Goliath! My King, the Lord is with me."

King Saul bowed his head. "The Lord was with me once, too," he whispered. The King stroked his beard and paced quickly back and forth. "Suit him up!" he cried.

The Israelite warriors laughed uproariously when they saw young David trying to stand up in the heavy armor. "I'll be quicker on my feet without armor," David said, silencing the crowd. "I must fight Goliath of Gath my own way."

The men were silent and respectfully let David pass by as he began the long walk into the valley to meet Goliath. Along the way, he chose five smooth stones from the dry river bed and held them tightly in his hand.

When Goliath saw the young boy approaching, he grew enraged. "You have sent a flea to fight the mighty Goliath?" he shouted at the Israelites. "You insult me!" Then he flung his spear at David. "Die Israelite!" he roared.

David leaped out of the way just in time. Goliath was bigger and stronger, but he was also slower. As Goliath drew his blade, David took one of his stones and put it in his sling. He twirled the sling faster and faster as he ducked and dodged Goliath's charges.

Then, running toward the giant, David hurled his stone. "Please, God, guide my aim!" he cried. It flew through the air and hit Goliath right between the eyes.

Goliath fell to the ground with an echoing thud. David won the battle! He killed the evil giant!

The Israelite soldiers cheered as the Philistines picked up their weapons and ran away. David led the army into the city, his brothers marching proudly behind him.

From that moment on, David became Israel's hero. He married Saul's daughter, Michal, and was crowned King after Saul died.

The city of Jerusalem became known as the "City of David." The people loved their King David. And so did God.